# The Many Faces of Grief

Written by Libby Kopec

Illustrated by Sarah K. Turner

Halo
PUBLISHING
INTERNATIONAL

ISBN: 978-1-63765-031-8
LCCN: 2021913811

Halo Publishing International, LLC
8000 W Interstate 10, Suite 600
San Antonio, Texas 78230
www.halopublishing.com

Printed and bound in the United States of America

To my loving and supportive husband, Dan, and our children, Delaney and Maddox. You are my biggest cheerleaders. Thank you for encouraging me to follow my dream and helping me to see that I can help more children and families through my writing. I love you forever and ever!

Dear Reader,

At some point, grief affects every family around the world. Even though we all have feelings of grief, we face grief in our own unique ways. There is no timeline for grief and there is no proper way to express grief. Everyone deals with grief in their own way and their own time. Grief is not pretty or perfect; it is messy and disorganized.

Elisabeth Kübler-Ross, psychiatrist and author, developed the five stages of grief to help people adjust to loss and change. When a person experiences grief, they may or may not go through all five stages: anger, depression, bargaining, acceptance, and denial. There is no correct order in working through these stages and it looks different every time.

You cannot plan for grief; sometimes it is unexpected and surprises you. Other times, grief grows as a situation gets worse. It is important to remember that you are not alone when you are grieving. There are people who care about you and want to support you. Be strong enough to let them support you; do not push people away. If you find that your grief is negatively affecting your life for a long period of time, then you need to talk about your feelings with a professional.

The best advice I have is to own your grief and allow yourself to feel the grief in whatever ways allow you to feel peace. The worst thing you can do is to ignore and bury the grief. This just prolongs the experience and causes grief to surprise you when you least expect it.

Please remember that everyone grieves differently and there is no proper way to grieve. Give yourself and your loved ones some grace when they are grieving and allow them to heal on their own time and in their own way.

With love,

Libby

# DEPRESSION

"Samesh! Time for bed!" his mother called out.

Samesh slowly crept to his bedroom to put on his pajamas. He then brushed his teeth and climbed into bed. His mother came in to say good night. "You haven't said much tonight. Are you okay? I know this move was unexpected, but I really think you will like it here if you give it a chance."

"How can I give it a chance when no one will talk to me at school?" cried Samesh. "Everyone ignores me because they already have their own group of friends. It is so lonely. I hate it here! I miss my friends back home! You just don't understand!"

"I know that everything is new for you and it can be scary. It is scary for me too," admitted his mom. "But you can't stop doing the things you love. You used to love playing chess after school and skating in the park. You are letting your sadness get in the way of new beginnings."

"How can I have new beginnings when I can't even be happy anymore. I have no one to play with and nothing to do when I get home from school" Samesh pouted.

"Maybe you need something to look forward to like your karate lessons. I heard there is a great place here in town and they are accepting new students. You could also join a club at school. That is a great place to meet new friends who are interested in the same things as you," suggested his mom.

"I did hear on the announcements that the Chess Club was meeting next Monday. I wonder if they would let me join in the middle of the year?" pondered Samesh.

"I'm sure they would be happy to have you join them. Who knows, maybe you might meet a few friends and then we can invite them over to hang out on the weekend. Would that make you happy?" his mom asked warmly.

"Yes, it would!" Samesh responded enthusiastically. It felt good to have a plan and he was looking forward to finding out more information about the Chess Club.

Have you ever felt lonely or felt like no one understands you?

Yes - What helped you feel better?

No - When Samesh was feeling depressed, he forgot how much he enjoyed karate lessons, playing chess, and skating in the park. What activities bring you joy?

# BARGAINING

Olivia threw her teddy bear across the room and screamed, "I want my old life back!" Everything she loved to do had been cancelled: her dance lessons, horseback riding, and visiting her Nana in the nursing home.

"Olivia, are you alright?" Her older sister Emma knocked on the door. "I heard you yelling. What is wrong?"

"Everything! This pandemic is ruining my life!" sobbed Olivia. Emma walked over and sat next to her on the bed. "Emma, do you think that if I just follow the rules and stop complaining that everything will go back to normal?"

Emma replied, "I don't think that is how this situation works. It is bigger than you and me. We cannot bargain our way out of this. We need to understand that our lives are never going to be the same. Some things have changed permanently and will never go back. Just remember that you are not alone in your grief, Olivia."

"I'm not?" asked Olivia.

"People all over the world have had to change their lives because of this pandemic. Many people have lost their jobs and had to move, schools have closed or are doing virtual learning, family members and friends have died, businesses and stores have shut down, and new rules are everywhere," Emma wisely stated. "We need to be grateful for what we have and what we can control."

"I know! Let's make a gratitude journal for you to write in every night. I bet it will make you feel better," suggested Emma. "What are some things you are grateful for right now?"

"Well, I am glad that I have Whiskers to cuddle with when I am sad. I also love using my art kit to create drawings and cards to send to grandma and her friends in the nursing home. And I am grateful that I have YOU as a big sister." Olivia smiled. "Thanks for helping me feel better."

Have you ever felt frustrated by life and all of life's rules?

Yes - What did you do to change your frustrated mood into a more positive mood?

No - Emma helped Olivia change her thinking and helped her create a more positive perspective. What can you suggest to someone to help them look at a situation in a more positive way?

# DENIAL

Cho's mother put her hands on his shoulders and asked, "How are you feeling?" They had learned that Cho's grandma was going to die soon. Cho loved his grandma and could not imagine life without her. Whenever his mom and dad tried to talk with him about the situation, Cho changed the subject or said, "Don't worry, she will get better." His parents knew that Cho was avoiding his big feelings by pretending that his grandma was fine.

Cho shrugged his shoulders and didn't respond. His mom squeezed him tight and said, "Cho, I think it is time you talk about your feelings. I made an appointment for you to talk with a counselor tomorrow."

"No way!" yelled Cho. "I don't want to tell a stranger about my feelings."

"I understand that you are scared. However, counselors are there to help people see the truth that is in front of them in a safe and caring way. Just give it a try," his mom suggested.

The next day, Cho went to talk with the counselor. Cho found that it was easy to talk with him. He asked Cho a lot of questions and even read Cho a book. It really helped Cho release his fear of his grandma dying.

After a couple of visits to the counselor, Cho understood that he could not avoid his grandma's sickness. She was going to die, and Cho needed to use the time he still had with her to share his love. He decided to write his grandma a love letter thanking her for all the sweet memories. The letter and his thoughtfulness put a smile on his grandma's face and created a happy memory that Cho will never forget.

Have you ever avoided your big feelings?

Yes - Looking back at that situation, how could you have dealt with your feelings differently?

No - Cho was burying his feelings and denying that he had them. This is common when people are dealing with grief. What questions could you ask Cho to encourage him to share his feelings?

# ANGER

Alina licked the last pieces of her honey cake off her fingers as she crossed the street to get her bike. She had gone to the local bakery after school to get a treat. When she walked up to the bike rack, she noticed two girls playing at the park. As she stared at them, the two girls looked at her, laughed, and started whispering. Alina felt tears swell up in her eyes as she grabbed her bike and started peddling home. Her frustration turned into anger the closer she got to home. By the time she walked through the front door, Alina felt like she was ready to punch someone. Her brother, Alexander, was in the kitchen getting a snack.

"Whoa! What is wrong with you?" Alexander asked after taking a quick look at her face.

"I just saw Yelena and Tatyana having fun together at the park and they were whispering and laughing at me." Alina slammed her fist down on the kitchen table. "Yelena was MY best friend!" screamed Alina. "I don't like Tatyana! She is mean and Yelena follows her everywhere. They keep secretly playing together and leaving me out. I just don't understand why this is happening?"

"I'm sorry Alina. Losing a friend is tough." Alexander said sympathetically. "I've had that happen to me before. Remember my friend Dimitri? We used to be best friends until Maxim moved in down the street."

"I forgot about that" replied Alina. "What ended up happening?"

"Well, we are no longer friends because Maxim was always putting me down and Dimitri wouldn't stick up for me. When I would tell Maxim to knock it off or to be nice, Dimitri kept telling me to stop causing trouble. As if I was the one who was the problem! I finally realized that it wasn't worth the hassle and I stopped hanging out with them," said Alexander. "Mom also gave me some good advice. She shared with me that some friends will only be your friend for a short time and most friendships don't last forever. This is why it is important to be kind and nice to everyone and not to focus on just one best friend."

Alina groaned loudly. She knew he was right, but it still hurt her heart to see them together.

"Hey, you need to find a way to calm down so you can think clearly. Maybe exercising would help? When I am mad I either do jumping jacks or push-ups to get the anger out of my body." Alexander stated. "Come on, let's do some jumping jacks together."

After about forty jumping jacks, Alina started to get tired. She realized that the anger was leaving her body. She made herself do ten more and then she collapsed on the floor. "Wow! That actually works!" she exclaimed. "Thanks, Alexander. I definitely feel less angry. I will have to remember this when I get upset at them again."

Have you ever felt so angry that you wanted to punch something?

Yes - Were you able to get rid of your anger in a positive way? What did you do?

No - Alina struggled to control her anger and therefore was giving away her power to the girls. What would you suggest to Alina to help her release her anger so she could keep her power and still feel good about herself?

# ACCEPTANCE

Noah looked at his dad's picture as he remembered saying goodbye to him six months ago. He had tightly hugged his dad that day knowing it was going to be a long time before they saw each other again. Noah's dad was in the army and had been called to active duty. This meant that his dad was stationed overseas while Noah and his mom remained in their hometown.

Noah missed seeing his dad every day. He missed throwing the football around the yard with his dad, watching their favorite television show together, and going to baseball games. His dad was the person he would turn to when he needed guidance and help. He always gave Noah good advice and would role play with him when Noah was nervous about trying something new. Now, everything felt different.

Luckily, Noah's teacher was understanding. She also had a dad in the military and had moved around a lot as a child. Noah often talked with her when he felt sad and missed his dad. She was the one who suggested keeping the picture of Noah and his dad next to his bed so that he could say good morning and good night to his dad every day. It helped him feel connected to his dad. Some days, Noah would hold the picture and tell his dad about his day and ask for advice on what to do with his problems. It was like having his dad right there with him.

Even though Noah missed seeing his dad every day, he understood that his grief would not last forever and he looked forward to his dad returning home.

Have you ever been apart from someone you love?

Yes – What helped you feel more connected to that person?

No – Noah was separated from his dad by distance. Some people are separated because of divorce, jail, work schedules, abuse, or neglect. What else can people do to feel connected to loved ones during these times?

# DEPRESSION

Sophia was feeling heartbroken because her grandpa had suddenly died, and she did not get the chance to say goodbye. Her Grandpa George was funny and kind. He always made people laugh with his corny jokes and silly faces. Sometimes he would make faces at Sophia to get her to giggle during dinner. Once she laughed so hard that she accidentally spit her beans all over the table. Another favorite memory was when he tried to play kickball with them. He kept missing the ball on purpose and falling on the ground. He was so silly! She really missed those fun times.

She decided to call her friend Lilly to cheer her up. "Lilly, my heart hurts and I cannot stop crying when I think of my grandpa," confessed Sophia. "My body hurts and I have had a headache for days. I don't know what to do."

"Your Grandpa George always made me laugh. Maybe we should look up some jokes," suggested Lilly. "I think he would like to see you smile and laugh."

"Great idea," said Sophia. "He really liked telling jokes at family gatherings."

"I found one!" exclaimed Lilly after scrolling through some jokes. "What did the right eye say to the left eye?"

"I don't know." said Sophia.

"Between us, something smells," Lilly answered while chuckling.

Both girls groaned in unison as they remembered the crazy jokes that Grandpa George would tell them. They went back and forth telling each other jokes for over twenty minutes. Finally, Sophia realized that she no longer felt heartbroken. Instead, she felt an immense feeling of love and warmth for her grandpa. Even though she would always miss him, she knew that the memories of their time together would keep his memory alive in her heart. Talking with Lilly about her feelings had really helped release the sadness from her body.

Have you ever had someone special die?

Yes - How did you deal with the sadness?

No - Having a loved one die not only affects our emotions, but it also affects our brains and bodies. Sophia was able to talk with her friend Lilly and ask for help. What else do you think would help someone who is feeling sad over losing a loved one?

# BARGAINING

Amir stared out the window of his classroom. He couldn't concentrate on his schoolwork. He kept thinking about his parents' divorce a few months ago. "Why did they have to fight so much?" he wondered. "Why couldn't they just get along and be friends?"

After class, Amir's teacher, Mr. Khan, pulled him aside to see what was wrong. Amir shared with him what was happening and that he really missed seeing his parents every day. The days he was with his dad, he missed his mom. The days he was at his mom's house, he missed his dad. He felt like he was always missing one of them. Amir thought that his parents' divorce was his fault. He felt like he ruined their relationship and caused them to be angry with each other. He wanted to talk with his parents and promise them that he would be a better son if they would get back together.

"Amir, your parents' divorce is not your fault. Your parents fighting has nothing to do with you. They fought because they had different opinions about how to live their lives. You can't bargain with them or fix their marriage. This is a grown-up situation," explained Mr. Khan.

"It isn't fair!" whined Amir. "Maleek's parents argue, and they are still married."

"Every relationship is different. You can't compare your life to Maleek's life. By you doing this, you are actually being unfair to yourself," replied Mr. Khan. He handed Amir a notebook and suggested that Amir write about his feelings since he felt it was so unfair. Mr. Khan knew that writing down your feelings helps you sort through the emotions and sometimes helps you think more clearly about the problem or situation.

After writing down his feelings about his new life, Amir realized that his parents' divorce wasn't his fault and that it was for the best. His parents were happier people away from each other. Amir could see that now and he was looking forward to his personal time with each parent.

Have you ever felt disappointed when something you wanted to happen didn't work out?

Yes – How did you handle it? Did you try and change the outcome?

No – Mr. Khan suggested that Amir write down his feelings about his new life. What do you think Amir wrote about in his notebook?

# DENIAL

Charlotte stared out of the bus window. She kept waiting to see Max pulling her mom down the street toward the bus stop. But her mom was already there, waiting alone. Max had been Charlotte's dog her entire life. He was so much more than a pet to Charlotte; he was her best friend. When Charlotte was feeling sad, Max would snuggle up with her and lick her tears away. They used to play for hours together. But over the last year, Max started to slow down and slept more often. He wasn't as playful as he used to be. Charlotte knew he was growing older, but she was unprepared for him to get sick and die. Her parents told her that Max had died while she was at school. She never even got to say goodbye to him. It didn't seem real.

As Charlotte and her mom walked home, her mom said, "Charlotte, tonight we are going to have a ceremony in honor of Max's life. I know you have been struggling with believing he is really gone."

"Mom, I keep hoping that he is still alive and will come back home. I love him so much and can't imagine my life without him," she sobbed.

"I understand," her mom gently said. "I think we all need to say goodbye to Max in our own way. Do you have any ideas of what you would like to do or say?"

"Yes," answered Charlotte, "I want to write a poem. We learned about poetry in school and how people use it to express their feelings. This will be perfect for the ceremony."

After dinner, Charlotte and her family gathered in the living room where Max used to sleep. They formed a circle and each person shared their memories and love of Max. Charlotte read her poem, her sister sang a song, her dad shared silly stories about Max when he was a puppy, and her mom had collected his special toys and put them in a decorated box. When the ceremony was over, Charlotte felt at peace. Even though Max was gone, he would always be her special dog.

Have you ever lost a pet that was special to you?

Yes - How did you feel when your pet died?

No - Charlotte's family had a ceremony to honor Max's life. What else could Charlotte's family have included in their ceremony?

# ANGER

Juan watched his teammates from the sideline. He felt left out and angry. Why did he have to trip over the stupid potted plant on the porch and break his ankle? "That is what I get for playing tag in the dark!" he thought. Now he couldn't play his favorite sport, soccer, until next season. Letting out a loud groan, Juan said, "Dad, I'm ready to leave."

His dad put his arm around him and asked, "It is frustrating having to watch your friends play without you, isn't it?"

"Yes!" replied Juan. "I just want to be out on the field scoring goals. It isn't fair!"

"Well, you are part of this team, even if you can't play right now. You owe it to your teammates to be here and to cheer them on," his dad said. "You seem tense. Let's take some deep breaths together. Breathwork can help boost your mood and calm down your nerves."

"That isn't going to help!" groaned Juan.

"Just try. Breathe in through your nose for four seconds, hold your breath for four seconds, and then exhale through your mouth for four seconds. Breathe in using your belly and try to get all of the air out of your lungs when you exhale. Do this at least five times and see how you feel," his dad directed.

"Fine!" huffed Juan as he rolled his eyes. He took a deep breath, held it, and then released it through his mouth. He counted in his head while he took his deep breaths. By the fifth breath, he was actually starting to feel a little calmer and not as angry. Maybe his dad was right.

"You're feeling better, aren't you?" his dad said. Juan nodded. "It's because your brain was craving oxygen. When we get upset and angry, we tend to breathe shallow. Therefore, we are not getting enough air and our body becomes stressed out. When we breathe deeply you are telling your body to calm down and relax."

"Wow, I didn't realize that breathing sent messages to my brain. Thanks, Dad!" exclaimed Juan. "I want to stay and cheer on my friends. After all, I am still part of the team."

Have you ever felt angry about something that you could no longer do?

Yes – What made you feel better?

No – Juan learns how his breathing can affect his mood. How do you feel after breathing five times like this? When can you use this breath work in your daily life?

# ACCEPTANCE

Isabella hopped up the stairs to her house. She couldn't wait to tell her mom about her day at school and the upcoming field trip. She pushed open the door, waved the permission slip in the air, and greeted her mom with a big, "Hello!" But her mom didn't answer. She was crying at the kitchen table with her head in her hands. "Mom, what is wrong?" Isabella asked.

Her mom pointed to a paper on the table. "We can't afford this apartment anymore. They are making us move out at the end of the month. Losing my job was the worst thing to ever happen to us!" sobbed her mom. "I never thought that I would lose my job. What are we going to do?"

Isabella quickly set down her backpack and ran over to hug her mom. Her heart sank as she realized that she wouldn't be able to go on her field trip after all.

Isabella was tired of not having enough money and missing out. Her friends went on amazing vacations, took numerous lessons, and had cool clothes. It was not fun being the poor kid. Isabella started to cry because she knew that the last three months had been hardest on her mom, and she could see that her mom was trying her best. She didn't want her mom to give up hope. Isabella took a deep breath and decided right then that she would encourage her mom to find a solution.

"Mom, don't worry. We will be okay, somehow we will be fine."

Her mom slowly raised her head and looked into Isabella's eyes. "How can you be so confident?" she questioned.

"Mom, you have always taught me to keep moving even if things get in my way. Right now, there is a huge obstacle in your way, so you need to move in another direction. I am sure there are other companies out there that need you." Isabella said. "Besides, you are hardworking, and in our family, we don't give up."

Her mom sighed, "You're right, honey. No matter what happens, we will be fine. I have to accept this situation and know that it is not forever." She paused for a moment and then said, "Thanks for the advice. I needed this gentle reminder. Your encouragement has helped me see what I need to do. Now, can you make us some tea? I need to make a list of everyone I know so I can start calling people tomorrow about potential jobs. There is no time to waste!"

Have you ever been worried about something big?

Yes – What did you do to resolve your worry? Who did you talk to about your worries?

No – After talking with Isabella, her mom felt hopeful and was able to accept her situation. She decided to take action in creating her new future. How can you take action in your life? What situations are you hoping to change?